JUST FOR YOU

JUST FOR YOU

The Fundamentals

STEVEN "POP" LEWIS, II

HARRIS AUTHOR SERVICES
Worldwide

Copyright © 2016 by Steven R. Lewis, II

Just for You: The Fundamentals

by Steven "POP" Lewis, II

Foreword by Horace Turnbull

Print ISBN: 978-0-692-70205-5
eBook ISBN: 978-0-692-70206-2

All rights reserved solely by the author. The author guarantees all contents are original and do not infringe upon the legal rights of any other person or work. No part of this publication may be reproduced or transmitted in any form or by any means without written permission by the author.

Visit us on the Web at: www.JourneyVerbage.com

Contents

Dedication	i
Foreword	iv
To My Grandsons	7
To My Beautiful Grandsons	10
Man Up!	13
I Apologize	14
No EXCUSES; Just ADJUSTMENTS	16
You Are Your Brother's Keeper	19
"You were created with VALUE."—Me	22
Know Who You Are	23

More Prayer. More Power.	25
Sharing Is Caring	27
"Money may leave you bankrupt, BUT good character will leave you a legacy."—Me	29
Choose Life	30
Good Work	32
Fail Forward	34
Patience Is a Virtue	36
"Until you BELIEVE in your DREAM, you are just WISHING."—Me	39
Hold On	40
Hope Floats	42
Keep Pushing	44
"If failure is an option, SUCCESS can't be."—Me	46
Think Win	47
Slow Down!	50
Walk It Out	53

Be Grateful	55
To the Reader	57
About the Author	59

Dedication

"A man is only as solid as his foundation."
—*Unknown*

Firstly, I want to thank God for choosing and trusting me with this awesome assignment from before the very foundation of the earth. I want to thank my parents, Steven Lewis and Cindy Valentine-Douglas, for determining to do the best they knew how and for never giving up on me. Special thanks to my sweet grandmothers, Mama and Nana (Sleep in Peace) for planting seeds of love that have nourished me along my journey.

To my bride, Tamari Lewis, you raised the bar high and challenged me to rise to it by

DEDICATION

"working the plan." I am eternally grateful to you, sweets. I love you, beautiful.

To the inspiration behind this book—my princes. Thayer M. Lewis and Jaxson C. Lewis, you are both rock stars: so smart, so handsome, so cool, and so full of love and talent. I pray that this book will challenge you to not settle for anything less than greatness. Never forget that great is not what you strive to be, it is who you are. You just have to believe it, trust it, and walk in that truth. I love you both to life!

Finally, to ALL my uncles, aunts, cousins, siblings, and friends, thank you for your support and prayers and just for LOVING me. To my prayer line brothers (Nation Builders) who prayed over me, my family, and this book, I am extremely grateful.

Without you all, I don't know where I would be.

Grace, peace, and love be unto you.

DEDICATION

Foreword

In the world in which we live, parents face the task of training and teaching their children how to obtain the overarching goal of living safe and productive lives. Because of the many challenges they face from dangers seen and unseen, it is a daunting and often difficult task. The task of giving our children a practical education through relating our own experiences and lessons learned, thereby creating for them a larger fund of information from which to draw when faced with making decisions, has seemingly been lost. Parents—fathers in particular—are so often too busy to give the consistent attention and guidance that is so critical to boys' development into men.

The sharing of experiences in our lives with our

FOREWORD

children (particularly our males) is invaluable in helping them to learn to process information, develop a healthy self-worth, and be able to make good decisions based on accurate information and the reality of their life situations.

In the following pages, a young father (with insights from others who love his sons) has begun this process of helping his sons in their development by providing for them a glimpse through his experiences, lessons learned, and what it's like to grow up. His experiences and lessons learned are not only for his boys but are also for all parents and their sons and daughters who are faced with the task of growing up.

Written by a proud father-in-law and grandpa.

To My Grandsons

The purpose of this note is to give you both some insight into life as I have experienced it: to hopefully keep you from running into the same pitfalls I have encountered that caused me pain and that I had to overcome.

Know God for yourself, and seek the truth with a humble heart, asking God to reveal Himself to you in a way that enables you to see and understand who He is. Love and protect each other, as your brother's family is everything and all you have. Always remember that you are representing your family name when you're out.

Seeking perfection is noble, but always remember

that perfection implies that you have reached the pinnacle and that there is nowhere else to go, no further growth, and nothing else to learn. Practice makes continued progress. You will always continue to grow and develop, so strive for continued progress. Remember that the moment you stop growing, you die.

In addition, the only free cheese is in the trap. Everybody wants something for nothing, but if it seems too good to be true, it probably is. Don't fall for anyone who appeals to your greed. If so, you will sell your gifts and talents for a bag of beans. Work hard for what you want; you won't place the same value on whatever you get for free.

Live life to the fullest, follow your dreams, do what makes you happy, and find a way to get paid for it. Make it your purpose to find out why God wakes you up each morning. It's not by chance; He has a plan for your life, so seek His wisdom to find out what that is.

I will leave you with the one piece of advice that I wish I had taken to heart most in my life. Procrastination is the thief of time. Don't talk about what you're going to do; do it and then talk about what you have done. Be men of your word: let your yes be yes and your no be no. Most importantly, when you have made it, find a way to reach down and pull someone up with you.

Love,
Pop Pop

To My Beautiful Grandsons

"Start children off on the way they should go, and even when they are old they will NOT turn from it."
—Proverbs 22:6, ESV

"So in everything, do to others what you would have them do to you, for this sums up the law and the prophets."
—Matthew 7:12, NIV

I don't know when you will read this or if someone will read it to you. First and foremost, I want you to know that I love you unconditionally. I will never stop loving you. I raised your father to respect his elders, peers, and especially women. So, with that being said, I am going to give you the same speech. Your elders are wise people, who, at one time in their lives, were YOU. You will eventually grow old, and the respect you show and give them now will shine back on you. The peers (friends) you choose will reflect on the type of person others will see you as. Choose them wisely. Your peers will respect and protect you, as you should them. Women are queens and should be treated with the utmost respect. They are not toys or property. They are your mom, grandmothers, sisters, aunts, cousins, and friends (peers).

Things I want you to always remember:

Put God first and the rest will fall into place.

To get respect, you must give (and show) respect.

Education is important; it is the one thing that cannot be taken away from you. Learn well.

Always smile; it costs nothing and will brighten someone else's day.

Lots of love,
Gee

Man Up!

I Apologize

"Boys hold others accountable. Men hold themselves accountable."
—Unknown

I apologize for not always hearing you out or considering your feelings. I apologize for forgetting that you have a mind of your own and what a BEAUTIFUL mind it is. With that mind, you have established your own point of view and opinions. I am often amazed by how extremely intelligent you are. So, I am sorry for not allowing you to express your thoughts sometimes. Sorry for making you feel like your opinions don't matter, because they DO. You MATTER to me, and I agree that you cannot always see that in my actions. ONE thing

I need you to understand is that I am human just like you, and I make mistakes. But a man should NEVER try to justify (look it up) his mistakes. Remember, a man holds himself accountable and makes the necessary adjustments to make sure he does not make the same mistake again. I promise you that I WILL do better because I LOVE you too much not to. Can you forgive me?

One day, I am going to have this dad thing down.

I PROMISE.

Love,
Me

No EXCUSES; Just ADJUSTMENTS

"Boys make excuses. Men make adjustments."
—Unknown

Dear Sons,

Listen closely. Being a man is a really big deal. HUGE! It is a lot of responsibility (look it up), and it carries a lot of expectations (look that up, too). The reason I am so tough on you boys sometimes is because, as your dad, my responsibility is to help get you guys ready to handle the weight of manhood. As a man, you are called to be the head of your family and a strong example of unconditional love, safety, and security. People will look up to you and look to you for advice. Your shoulders will be tired from carrying the burdens of others at times. The pressures of manhood will drive you to tears sometimes, baby boys. You will have to work, run a business, earn money, and learn how to invest that money wisely. As a man, you have to read and study to obtain knowledge and then learn how to use that knowledge in a productive way. You will have to surround yourself with people who are going to challenge you to do and be better.

Tired yet?

One thing a man should NEVER do, however, is make EXCUSES for not taking on the challenge of his manhood. Growing into manhood is HARD WORK, and many will never graduate to manhood because they do not want to step up to the challenge. They make EXCUSES instead. PLEASE don't let this be you, baby boys. Excuses are very harmful to your GREATNESS. I want you to become men who make the necessary ADJUSTMENTS (changes) instead of excuses. I want you to become men who step up to the challenges of manhood and make up in your mind that you are going to WIN!

So, in the meantime, be humble, get information, apply the information, watch, learn, and listen. I am so EXCITED about the MEN you are becoming!

Say it with me one more time: NO EXCUSES. JUST ADJUSTMENTS.

Love,
Me

You Are Your Brother's Keeper

"A person standing alone can be attacked and defeated, but two can stand back-to-back and conquer. Three are even better, for a triple-braided cord is not easily broken."
—Ecclesiastes 4:12, NLT

Dear Sons,

Nothing should ever come between brothers. A rope with many cords is strong and not easily broken. Listen, you don't always, nor will you always, agree with each other. You won't always see eye to eye. You are going to fight, argue, and be mad at each other. You have different personalities (look it up), different understandings, and different perspectives (look it up). This is what makes each of you so SPECIAL. For this reason, you will not always see things the same way. But PLEASE don't allow your unique (look that up, too) points of view to build a wall between you. You are all the other has, so you HAVE to make your brotherhood work. Learn to talk through the things you don't agree with, fight if you have to, but get back to LOVING each other as fast as possible. Baby boys, tomorrow is not promised to ANYONE. You never want to regret not saying "I'm sorry," "I FORGIVE you," or "I love you" to each other. You boys have to love each other enough not to let disagreements, jealousy, girls, or anything else for that matter break your brotherly bond. It's a beautiful thing seeing you work together, play together, and help each other out. That makes my heart smile. There is strength in numbers, might in unity, and power in love.

Love,
Me

"You were created with VALUE."–Me

Know Who You Are

"But you are a CHOSEN people, a ROYAL priesthood, a HOLY nation, a people belonging to God."
—1 Peter 2:9, NIV

Dear Sons,

I want you to memorize this scripture. If you ever have any questions about who you are, look NO further!

No matter what ANYBODY says, this is what your CREATOR says about you. You are so very unique (look it up). God has carved out a special place in the UNIVERSE that can be filled only by you, sons. That is how important you are to God. So don't worry about FITTING IN, because you were created to STAND OUT. Please always remember that you ARE royalty, you ARE chosen, and you ARE holy (set apart). So do your dad a HUGE favor: don't be afraid to believe who you have been created to be. NO ONE in this world can be YOU or quite like you, nor can anyone do what you have been CALLED to do. You are GIFTS to the universe. NEVER forget it!

Love,
Me

More Prayer. More Power.

"A man who stays on his knees can stand through anything."
—Unknown

Dear Sons,

When in doubt, pray. When you are unsure, pray. When you don't have the answers to life's most difficult questions, pray. Prayer has been my weapon of choice to fight life's battles, and it has not failed me yet! Prayer gives you the opportunity to let go of the pressures of life and leave them with someone who is so much more equipped to handle them. As strong as you are, sons, it's OK to be vulnerable (look it up) at times. It's OK to admit that you need help, and it's OK to ask for help. Do not allow circumstances in life to steal your joy and happiness. You are a royal priesthood, a holy generation set apart to do GREAT work. Challenges, confusion, and falling short of reaching your goals come with the process. You are on the road to greatness, and, unfortunately, it's not an easy road to travel. Let prayer be your navigation system.

Love,
Me

Sharing Is Caring

"Talent is God given. Be Humble.
Fame is man given. Be Grateful.
Conceit is self-given. Be Careful."
—John Wooden

Dear Sons,

OK so, you guys are talented, intelligent, powerful, God-loving, not to mention VERY handsome dudes! You get it honest (LOL)! Embrace these qualities because God gave them to you. Be proud of who you are, enjoy who you are, love who you are . . .

BUT I challenge you to love others the same way

you love yourself. Be willing to share your gifts with the world. Don't be selfish with your God-given talents, because they were not given to you just for you. They were given to you to fulfill a need in someone else's life. You have a golden opportunity to be a part of something SO much bigger than you. Don't limit yourself by focusing only on yourself. You have to think BIGGER and BROADER; God has HUGE plans for you, baby boys, and it makes my heart skip a beat when I think about it. There is a special place in the universe that is carved out for your skills, talents, and gifts. You have a responsibility to the universe to fill that void. The world is counting on you.

Love,
Me

"Money may leave you bankrupt, BUT good character will leave you a legacy." –Me
___

Choose Life

"This day I call the heavens and the earth as witnesses against you that I have set before you life and death, blessings and curses. Now CHOOSE life, so that you and your children may live..."
—Deuteronomy 30:19, NIV

Dear Sons,

Life is a sum (look it up) total of the choices you make. There is such a thing as right and wrong, boys; never forget that. I need you to understand that the ability to choose is a gift. It is a privilege that should not be taken lightly. In fact, the choice to do right or wrong will determine the path your life will take, depending on which one you choose.

Life and death and blessings and curses are linked to your choices, sons. Please always remember that you have the unlimited POWER to choose right, even though, truth be told, right is often the hardest thing to choose. But you CAN do it! You are blessed and favored by God. You are KINGS, and anyone who tells you differently is a LIAR!

Greatness is upon you, sons. I am SOOO proud of you.

Love,
Me

Good Work

"And let us not grow weary of doing good, for in due season we will reap, if we do not give up."
—Galatians 6:9, NLT

Dear Sons,

Don't get tired of doing good. And I don't mean doing good because you want something in return. I challenge you to do good because that's just the right thing to do. There are people who you may come across who just need your smile or a nice word, or they may just need someone to listen to them. Be the person who fulfills a need, and, by default (look it up), your needs will be met as well. For in due season, you will reap IF you don't give up. You can't quit sharing what God has blessed you with. The more you give, the more room you have to get. See how this works?

Last thing: understand that not everyone has a giving spirit; some just like to take. Please don't allow these types of people to steal your desire to help others in any way you can. You pray for them, but don't let them mistake your kindness for weakness. Stay true to you, use your head AND your heart, and you will be just fine.

Love,
Me

Fail Forward

"Failures, repeated failures, are finger posts on the road to achievement. One fails forward towards success."
—C.S. Lewis

Dear Sons,

Failure is only permanent if you are committed to making it so. Success can blind you to things to which failure will bring your attention. The bottom line is that you have a choice (there goes that "C" word again). People who are successful fail forward, meaning they fail as they are pressing forward toward their dreams. They use their failure as fuel to power their dreams. You learn some valuable lessons from failure. You learn to look at what you could have done better and to make adjustments. It gives you a road map for what to do differently. Failure gives you motivation and inspiration to work harder so that you don't fail the same way again. Life is a process of falling down and learning how to get back up, sons. You get SMARTER during the getting up, you get BETTER during the getting up, you get STRONGER during the getting up, and you get WISER during the getting up. Don't be afraid to try new things, don't be afraid to give all you have, don't be afraid to take some "calculated" (look it up) risks, and don't be afraid to go after your dreams and what God has called you to do. Walk by faith and not by sight, and failure will never define you.

Love,
Me

Patience Is a Virtue

"For I know the plans I have for you," declares the Lord, "plans to prosper you and not to harm you, plans to give you hope and a future."
—Jeremiah 29:11, NIV

"Patience is the ability to count down before you blast off."
—Unknown

Dear Sons,

The best thing you will EVER develop in life is patience—the ability to wait, to understand that some things just won't happen right now, tomorrow, or even this year. One of the reasons I tell you "NO" sometimes (OK, a lot of times! LOL) or "not right now" is because I need you to develop an appreciation for waiting. I need you to understand that things in life will not always come when you want them to come. People are not going to drop everything they are doing to get you what you want at the time you want it. The world—and life—doesn't work that way, baby boys. Sometimes, the things we want have a time frame that does not match up with ours, and we have to learn to be cool with that. Please also understand that "not now" does not mean "no." It just means to wait; there may be a lesson that you need to learn while you wait. So, do me a HUGE favor! Be patient in school; wait for the teacher to show you the formula. Be patient with your brothers and sisters; they won't always understand what you are trying to say. Be patient in your boyhood because being a man is a really BIG responsibility, and you have a lot to learn. Be patient with your mom; she just wants what is best for you. Be patient with wins, losses, disappointments, and delays; all these things develop the muscles that make you stronger. Be patient with your dreams; they will take time to build, but they will come true only if you WORK while you wait. Lastly, be patient with me. I love you too much not to give you ALL this information, so, make sure you read ALL of it!

Love,
Me

"Until you BELIEVE in your DREAM, you are just WISHING." –Me

Hold On

"Your purpose is what you were created for. Your gifts are the ingredients purpose needs to come together and the oven is what purpose needs to come alive."
—Inspiration

Dear Sons,

Great things don't always happen overnight; they take TIME. You can't take cake mix out of the cabinet, open the box, eat it, and say you are eating cake. That cake mix does not become a cake until it goes through the PROCESS of becoming the cake. You have to add eggs, butter, and milk to the mix (INGREDIENTS), then you have to heat up the oven and put the mixed ingredients in the oven. The crazy thing about this cake-making process is that the cake only becomes ready to eat after it has undergone the HEAT of the oven. The cake had to go through an uncomfortable (look it up) period in order for it to be ready to come into its PURPOSE. You will have plenty of "OVEN" experiences in your life, and some will be hotter than others. PLEASE always remember that the heat is necessary for God to bring purpose out of you. It will not be easy; life is not always sweet. PRACTICE thanking God in the good times so it will be all you know how to do in the bad times. PLEASE PLEASE PLEASE hold on and trust the process.

Love,
Me

Hope Floats

"Faith is the confidence that what we hope for will actually happen; it gives us assurance about things we cannot see."
—Hebrews 11:1, NLT

Dear Sons,

This may seem crazy, but at some point in your lives, baby boys, you are going to have to believe in things you can't see. There will come a time in your life where your hope (look it up) will be leaning on something that at that moment may not exist. It is in these moments that I need you to believe the most, baby boys. Hope is like a hidden treasure: not many people find it, and the ones who do don't always hold on to it. Hope is tricky, sons; its complicated (look it up), and it's hard sometimes to hang onto it. But what I found is that it takes a special person to dance with the uncertainties (look this up, too) of hope. A person with faith (another one to look up) must also have an imagination, a tight grip, and a strong desire to work in order to turn their hope into reality. All of this and more describes the type of young men you are becoming. I can't tell you how HOPEFUL that makes me feel.

Love,
Me

Keep Pushing

"Ambition is the path to success. Persistence is the vehicle you arrive in."
—Bill Bradley

Dear Sons,

Persistence is determination—staying POWER . . . the desire to KEEP GOING! Life is one of the most painfully rewarding experiences you will ever have. STRUGGLE is necessary, PAIN won't last, and FEAR is a lie. You have an assignment—a very special job to do. But you MUST understand that life is NOT FAIR! No one is going to give you anything. It is no one else's responsibility to give you anything. There will be people who are going to disappoint you. There will be situations that won't turn out the way you thought they would. There will be times when you feel like giving up on your assignment because the weight of it seems too heavy to carry. BUT I need you to KEEP GOING! If you focus only on the pain, if you focus only on the disappointment, if you focus only on the outcome, sons, you will NEVER grow. I challenge you to get a reward from the pain, get a reward from the disappointment, and learn from the outcome. It won't be easy, but it will DEFINITELY be worth it.

Love,
Me

"If failure is an option, SUCCESS can't be." —Me

———

Think Win

"For as he thinketh in his heart, so is he..."
—Proverbs 23:7, KJV

"Winners win. Losers lose."
—Dr. Eric Thomas

Dear Sons,

Winners choose to win, and losers choose to lose. One of the biggest differences between winners and losers is the way they think. What you think of YOU is, at some point, going to become who YOU are. What you choose to listen to and look at will have a HUGE impact on your thinking. Who you choose to hang out with or who you choose to surround yourself with will affect the way you think. And how you think, baby boys, will make you winners or losers. It will transform you or destroy you. But the choice is yours! If I could give you some strong, loving, fatherly advice, I would recommend that you surround yourself with winners. Listen and watch winners, study how winners think, and apply what you learn to your life. Let me define a winner. A winner is someone who puts God first. Winners take care of their families. Winners are obsessed (look it up) with self-assessment, self-improvement, and self-growth. Winners are consistent (faithful) in small things. Winners stay true to who they are, trust the process, and never give up on their dreams. Winners love people and are willing to make sacrifices to help who they can when they can. Winners are humble. Winners are grateful. Winners don't settle for losing. Winners are problem solvers. Winners do not let fear stop them from reaching their goals; instead, they use fear to feed their goals. Winners don't expect anyone to do for them what they should be doing for themselves. Winners are go-getters. Winners know what they want and NEVER settle for less.

Winners learn from their failures and mistakes. Winners choose to be better. A winner does not make excuses—only adjustments. A winner reads, studies, and masters information. A winner attracts other winners. Winners change the game. Winners change the WORLD. Losers do the complete opposite.

Choose wisely.

Love,
Me

Slow Down!

"Trials are just seasons that prepare us for our destiny. Just like fall, spring, summer and winter, they pass. Whatever the trial is, it has to pass."
—Unknown

"Sometimes, standing still is the best way to move forward."
—Me

Dear Sons,

Be careful not to miss your blessing because you are moving too fast. Life has ups and downs, periods of rapid movement and steady flow, and seasons of drought. In dry seasons, it seems like nothing is moving and everything has stopped growing. It is in these moments that you will feel the most anxious (look it up). You are going to feel the desire to DO something: to force something to move or some action to happen or to speed up a process. But I am advising you to STOP right there at that moment. Wait a minute, breathe, relax, and reflect (look it up). Scripture encourages us to be anxious for NOTHING, but in all things, through prayer and thanksgiving, make your request known unto God. I have had many dry seasons, and because I didn't understand them, I have made MANY mistakes. I was not mature enough to wait. It took me a long time to accept that sometimes doing something doesn't mean you are doing the right thing. Sometimes, God needs you to sit still while He teaches you some new things, opens up new opportunities for you, and develops in you the character (there goes that word again!) that you need to be successful in the place He is preparing for you. Sometimes, you have to go through the desert to get to your promise. Hang in there, *you gone be ALRIGHT!* I promise.

Love,
Me

Walk It Out

"Trust in the Lord with all your heart, and lean not on your own understanding; in all your ways submit to him, and he will make your paths straight."
—Proverbs 3:5–6, NIV

Dear Sons,

There will be times in your life, sons, that will look and feel like there is no way around or out of them. Murphy's Law says that whatever can go wrong will go wrong. You won't always understand why, it won't always make sense, and it won't be comfortable. But it will be worth it if you learn from it. There is ALWAYS a way out; sometimes, you just have to be PATIENT and WAIT on your exit. But your way of escape will always arrive as long as you are careful not to lean on your own understanding. What things appear to be may not be what they really are. Things that challenge you the most might be the exact things that you need to save your life. Weird, right? Don't think you have to figure everything out; our smart brains are not always enough, and our emotions can lie to us. Life is a great teacher, and you can only lose in life if you don't learn from it. A good man's steps are ordered by the Lord. Trust the process.

Love,
Me

Be Grateful

/'grātfəl/

"Feeling or showing an appreciation of kindness; thankful..."
—The Oxford Pocket Dictionary of Current English. 2009.

To the Reader

I am grateful. If you have reached this page, then you have either read all the way through the book or skipped to the very last page (LOL!). If you have read the book all the way to this page, thank you from the bottom of my heart. I pray that the principles in this book will find the appropriate space in your heart and mind. Hopefully, this is a game changer or even a solid starting point for you. Please always remember that applied information changes situations. So, my challenge to you is to use what you have learned from this book and to walk fearlessly into the greatness that awaits you. And for those who skipped to the last page, I challenge you to read the book and apply the above lessons!

I love you all with the love of Jesus Christ, my Lord and Savior.

Grace and Peace,
Steven "POP" Lewis

PSST! There's much, much more to come. Stay tuned...

About the Author

Steven Robert Lewis, II is a young millennial who has a passion and love for people. This husband and father has been in public service for over 13 years and is convinced that he is operating in his life calling. He has a special place in his heart for the empowerment of teenagers and young adults. This demographic has been his focus for the past nine years. His approach is reality focused, designed not only to open the eyes of his

ABOUT THE AUTHOR

listeners to their own unlimited potential but also, most importantly, to spur them onto a determined plan for full action. Steven Lewis is a speaker, teacher, author, and, most importantly, a humble servant of the Most High God.

www.ingramcontent.com/pod-product-compliance
Lightning Source LLC
Chambersburg PA
CBHW072108290426
44110CB00014B/1863